Scripture Study Journal

TOPICS

This Journal Belongs To

My Journal Volume

Date I Began this Journal

Date I Completed this Journal

- This journal is meant to help you in your scripture studying of various TOPICS
- It is designed to :
- 1- Help you to organize your studies and help you to find things easily
- 2- Help you to reference your writings with other journals you have, or will have
- 3- Help you dig and discover as you study your scriptures
- This journal focuses on studying individual TOPICS (doctrines and principles)
- We also have available for you a journal that helps you study individual chapters. The journals are similar in nature and have places where you can reference to each other.
  - For example, if you have a page in this journal titled "FAITH, and in your other journal you study a chapter in your scriptures that teaches a lot about "FAITH", there are places on pages in each journal where you can link it to each other.
  - You may have noticed that on the first page of this journal there is a place where you can determine what "volume" that journal is. We recommend that you start this journal as volume one and the next journal as volume two, and so on.
  - When you link from journal to journal, your references can look something like: "See also Volume 1, page 24" or even easier: "1:24". Then you go to volume 1, page 24, and link *back* to the page you just wrote that reference on! Now your writings are organized and will be so easy to find!
- On page 3 of this journal you have a TABLE OF CONTENTS so you can keep an organized record of where you can find the topics that you have studied and written about.
- On each page in your journal you have various boxes with places you can record things. Here are some ways you can use those boxes:
- **DEFINITION**: Here you can write some definitions or explanations for the topic you are studying.
  - Example: *FAITH:*
    - *Complete trust or confidence in God.*
    - *Faith grows as we act and feed the faith we have. Like a seed.*
- **SCRIPTURES**: In this box you can keep a record of some of your favorite places in the scriptures that teach about the doctrine or principle you are studying. You can write the reference (where to find it) in the left column, and an explanation of what it teaches you about your topic in the right column (you can choose to quote the scripture or paraphrase what it is teaching you).

James 2:17	Faith alone, without works (actions), is dead... or not alive.

- **FAVORITE QUOTES**: In this box you can keep several quotes about your topic. Write small!! You can fill this up really fast!
- **OTHER JOURNALS I HAVE WRITTEN ABOUT THIS TOPIC**: This box is intended to help you link to other journals you have. So, if you write about FAITH on pages 4 and 5 in this journal, and also on pages 28 and 29 in this journal, you can link those pages together in this box. Also, as explained above, if you fill up this journal and have multiple volumes, you can link all your volumes together in this box. Then, if you are going to give a talk, lesson or devotional on this topic you have all of your hours of study easily available to you!
- **MY PERSONAL THOUGHTS AND INSIGHTS:** This box is intended for you to write and write your own thoughts about this subject. Here you can write personal experiences, insights, questions, your personal testimony, etc. You can draw pictures, make diagrams, make outlines... there are so many possibilities!
- For more ideas and examples on how to use this journal, and **A LIST OF SUGGESTED TOPICS** come to www.theredheadedhostess.com

My Table of Contents

Page Numbers	Topics

Page Numbers	Topics

Doctrine/Principle

Definition:

Scriptures that Teach this Doctrine / Principle

Scripture Reference:	What it teaches

Favorite Quotes

Other Journals I have written about this topic:

My Personal Thoughts and Insights

Doctrine/Principle

Definition:

Scriptures that Teach this Doctrine / Principle

Scripture Reference:	What it teaches

Favorite Quotes

Other Journals I have written about this topic:

My Personal Thoughts and Insights

Doctrine/Principle

Definition:

Scriptures that Teach this Doctrine / Principle

Scripture Reference:	What it teaches

Favorite Quotes

Other Journals I have written about this topic:

My Personal Thoughts and Insights

Doctrine/Principle

Definition:

Scriptures that Teach this Doctrine / Principle

Scripture Reference:	What it teaches

Favorite Quotes

Other Journals I have written about this topic:

My Personal Thoughts and Insights

Doctrine/Principle

Definition:

Scriptures that Teach this Doctrine / Principle

Scripture Reference:	What it teaches

Favorite Quotes

Other Journals I have written about this topic:

My Personal Thoughts and Insights

Doctrine/Principle

Definition:

Scriptures that Teach this Doctrine / Principle

Scripture Reference:	What it teaches

Favorite Quotes

Other Journals I have written about this topic:

My Personal Thoughts and Insights

My Personal Thoughts and Insights

Doctrine/Principle

Definition:

Scriptures that Teach this Doctrine / Principle

Scripture Reference:	What it teaches

Favorite Quotes

Other Journals I have written about this topic:

My Personal Thoughts and Insights

- -

Doctrine/Principle

Definition:

Scriptures that Teach this Doctrine / Principle

Scripture Reference:	What it teaches

Favorite Quotes

Other Journals I have written about this topic:

My Personal Thoughts and Insights

My Personal Thoughts and Insights

Doctrine/Principle

Definition:

Scriptures that Teach this Doctrine / Principle

Scripture Reference:	What it teaches

Favorite Quotes

Other Journals I have written about this topic:

My Personal Thoughts and Insights

Doctrine/Principle

Definition:

Scriptures that Teach this Doctrine / Principle

Scripture Reference:	What it teaches

Favorite Quotes

Other Journals I have written about this topic:

My Personal Thoughts and Insights

Doctrine/Principle

Definition:

Scriptures that Teach this Doctrine / Principle

Scripture Reference:	What it teaches

Favorite Quotes

Other Journals I have written about this topic:

My Personal Thoughts and Insights

My Personal Thoughts and Insights

Doctrine/Principle

Definition:

Scriptures that Teach this Doctrine / Principle

Scripture Reference:	What it teaches

Favorite Quotes

Other Journals I have written about this topic:

My Personal Thoughts and Insights

Doctrine/Principle

Definition:

Scriptures that Teach this Doctrine / Principle

Scripture Reference:	What it teaches

Favorite Quotes

Other Journals I have written about this topic:

My Personal Thoughts and Insights

My Personal Thoughts and Insights

30

Doctrine/Principle

Definition:

Scriptures that Teach this Doctrine / Principle

Scripture Reference:	What it teaches

Favorite Quotes

Other Journals I have written about this topic:

My Personal Thoughts and Insights

Doctrine/Principle

Definition:

Scriptures that Teach this Doctrine / Principle

Scripture Reference:	What it teaches

Favorite Quotes

Other Journals I have written about this topic:

My Personal Thoughts and Insights

Doctrine/Principle

Definition:

Scriptures that Teach this Doctrine / Principle

Scripture Reference:	What it teaches

Favorite Quotes

Other Journals I have written about this topic:

35

My Personal Thoughts and Insights

My Personal Thoughts and Insights

Doctrine/Principle

Definition:

Scriptures that Teach this Doctrine / Principle

Scripture Reference:	What it teaches

Favorite Quotes

Other Journals I have written about this topic:

My Personal Thoughts and Insights

My Personal Thoughts and Insights

Doctrine/Principle

Definition:

Scriptures that Teach this Doctrine / Principle

Scripture Reference:	What it teaches

Favorite Quotes

Other Journals I have written about this topic:

My Personal Thoughts and Insights

Doctrine/Principle

Definition:

Scriptures that Teach this Doctrine / Principle

Scripture Reference:	What it teaches

Favorite Quotes

Other Journals I have written about this topic:

My Personal Thoughts and Insights

Doctrine/Principle

Definition:

Scriptures that Teach this Doctrine / Principle

Scripture Reference:	What it teaches

Favorite Quotes

Other Journals I have written about this topic:

My Personal Thoughts and Insights

Doctrine/Principle

Definition:

Scriptures that Teach this Doctrine / Principle

Scripture Reference:	What it teaches

Favorite Quotes

Other Journals I have written about this topic:

My Personal Thoughts and Insights

Doctrine/Principle

Definition:

Scriptures that Teach this Doctrine / Principle

Scripture Reference:	What it teaches

Favorite Quotes

Other Journals I have written about this topic:

My Personal Thoughts and Insights

- -

Doctrine/Principle

Definition:

Scriptures that Teach this Doctrine / Principle

Scripture Reference:	What it teaches

Favorite Quotes

Other Journals I have written about this topic:

My Personal Thoughts and Insights

Doctrine/Principle

Definition:

Scriptures that Teach this Doctrine / Principle

Scripture Reference:	What it teaches

Favorite Quotes

Other Journals I have written about this topic:

My Personal Thoughts and Insights

Doctrine/Principle

Definition:

Scriptures that Teach this Doctrine / Principle

Scripture Reference:	What it teaches

Favorite Quotes

Other Journals I have written about this topic:

My Personal Thoughts and Insights

Doctrine/Principle

Definition:

Scriptures that Teach this Doctrine / Principle

Scripture Reference:	What it teaches

Favorite Quotes

Other Journals I have written about this topic:

My Personal Thoughts and Insights

My Personal Thoughts and Insights

Doctrine/Principle

Definition:

Scriptures that Teach this Doctrine / Principle

Scripture Reference:	What it teaches

Favorite Quotes

Other Journals I have written about this topic:

My Personal Thoughts and Insights

My Personal Thoughts and Insights

Doctrine/Principle

Definition:

Scriptures that Teach this Doctrine / Principle

Scripture Reference:	What it teaches

Favorite Quotes

Other Journals I have written about this topic:

My Personal Thoughts and Insights

Doctrine/Principle

Definition:

Scriptures that Teach this Doctrine / Principle

Scripture Reference:	What it teaches

Favorite Quotes

Other Journals I have written about this topic:

My Personal Thoughts and Insights

Doctrine/Principle

Definition:

Scriptures that Teach this Doctrine / Principle

Scripture Reference:	What it teaches

Favorite Quotes

Other Journals I have written about this topic:

My Personal Thoughts and Insights

My Personal Thoughts and Insights

Doctrine/Principle

Definition:

Scriptures that Teach this Doctrine / Principle

Scripture Reference:	What it teaches

Favorite Quotes

Other Journals I have written about this topic:

My Personal Thoughts and Insights

66

Doctrine/Principle

Definition:

Scriptures that Teach this Doctrine / Principle

Scripture Reference:	What it teaches

Favorite Quotes

Other Journals I have written about this topic:

My Personal Thoughts and Insights

Doctrine/Principle

Definition:

Scriptures that Teach this Doctrine / Principle

Scripture Reference:	What it teaches

Favorite Quotes

Other Journals I have written about this topic:

My Personal Thoughts and Insights

Doctrine/Principle

Definition:

Scriptures that Teach this Doctrine / Principle

Scripture Reference:	What it teaches

Favorite Quotes

Other Journals I have written about this topic:

My Personal Thoughts and Insights

Doctrine/Principle

Definition:

Scriptures that Teach this Doctrine / Principle

Scripture Reference:	What it teaches

Favorite Quotes

Other Journals I have written about this topic:

My Personal Thoughts and Insights

My Personal Thoughts and Insights

Doctrine/Principle

Definition:

Scriptures that Teach this Doctrine / Principle

Scripture Reference:	What it teaches

Favorite Quotes

Other Journals I have written about this topic:

My Personal Thoughts and Insights

Doctrine/Principle

Definition:

Scriptures that Teach this Doctrine / Principle

Scripture Reference:	What it teaches

Favorite Quotes

Other Journals I have written about this topic:

My Personal Thoughts and Insights

Doctrine/Principle

Definition:

Scriptures that Teach this Doctrine / Principle

Scripture Reference:	What it teaches

Favorite Quotes

Other Journals I have written about this topic:

My Personal Thoughts and Insights

My Personal Thoughts and Insights

Doctrine/Principle

Definition:

Scriptures that Teach this Doctrine / Principle

Scripture Reference:	What it teaches

Favorite Quotes

Other Journals I have written about this topic:

My Personal Thoughts and Insights

Doctrine/Principle

Definition:

Scriptures that Teach this Doctrine / Principle

Scripture Reference:	What it teaches

Favorite Quotes

Other Journals I have written about this topic:

My Personal Thoughts and Insights

My Personal Thoughts and Insights

Doctrine/Principle

Definition:

Scriptures that Teach this Doctrine / Principle

Scripture Reference:	What it teaches

Favorite Quotes

Other Journals I have written about this topic:

My Personal Thoughts and Insights

Doctrine/Principle

Definition:

Scriptures that Teach this Doctrine / Principle

Scripture Reference:	What it teaches

Favorite Quotes

Other Journals I have written about this topic:

My Personal Thoughts and Insights

Doctrine/Principle

Definition:

Scriptures that Teach this Doctrine / Principle

Scripture Reference:	What it teaches

Favorite Quotes

Other Journals I have written about this topic:

My Personal Thoughts and Insights

Doctrine/Principle

Definition:

Scriptures that Teach this Doctrine / Principle

Scripture Reference:	What it teaches

Favorite Quotes

Other Journals I have written about this topic:

My Personal Thoughts and Insights

Doctrine/Principle

Definition:

Scriptures that Teach this Doctrine / Principle

Scripture Reference:	What it teaches

Favorite Quotes

Other Journals I have written about this topic:

My Personal Thoughts and Insights

Doctrine/Principle

Definition:

Scriptures that Teach this Doctrine / Principle

Scripture Reference:	What it teaches

Favorite Quotes

Other Journals I have written about this topic:

My Personal Thoughts and Insights

My Personal Thoughts and Insights

Doctrine/Principle

Definition:

Scriptures that Teach this Doctrine / Principle

Scripture Reference:	What it teaches

Favorite Quotes

Other Journals I have written about this topic:

My Personal Thoughts and Insights

My Personal Thoughts and Insights

Doctrine / Principle

Definition:

Scriptures that Teach this Doctrine / Principle

Scripture Reference:	What it teaches

Favorite Quotes

Other Journals I have written about this topic:

My Personal Thoughts and Insights

My Personal Thoughts and Insights

Doctrine/Principle

Definition:

Scriptures that Teach this Doctrine / Principle

Scripture Reference:	What it teaches

Favorite Quotes

Other Journals I have written about this topic:

My Personal Thoughts and Insights

My Personal Thoughts and Insights

Made in the USA
San Bernardino, CA
26 October 2015